ALLISON VAN WHEELER

blissfully unaware

First edition

ISBN: 9798862104424

This book was professionally typeset on Reedsy.
Find out more at reedsy.com

to everyone who said I couldn't do it,
look at me now

Contents

the sun

I spend my days chasing the sun,
   But I just end up getting spun
   Spinning around, getting dizzy
   Just trying to stay busy.

As I find my way back to earth
   I realize just how much it's worth.
   The exhaustion and pain,
   With little to gain.

That is when I make the decision,
   To no longer make any revisions.
   I live my life for me,
   With that, I will always be free.

we come from the sky

It is the first of October, and I am dazed
  by the colors of leaves, their red and gold
  still shimmering in the afternoon sun.
  I have been thinking about a line in my favorite poem—We
come from the sky—and I realize it is not really true.
  We come from the ground, as trees do, or as stars do,
  from the earth that is our mother and our grave.

rainbow

In hues that dance on stormy skies,
A spectrum born when darkness flies.
A canvas painted, bold and bright,
The promise whispered in the light.

Through raindrops falling, silver tears,
A symphony of hopes and fears.
The storm may rage, the clouds may weep,
Yet in the heart, a promise deep.

A rainbow born from sun and rain,
A tapestry of joy and pain.
Each color tells a tale untold,
In every hue, a dream unfolds.

Red, the fire of passion's flame,
Orange, warmth that has no name.

Yellow, like the sun's embrace,
Chasing shadows, leaving no trace.

Green, the whispers of nature's call,
Blue, a calm that covers all.
Indigo, the twilight's kiss,
Violet, the dreams we wish.

Hope, a bridge of colors bright,
Spanning from the day to night.
In every storm, a promise true,
A rainbow's grace, a sky so new.

So when the world feels dark and gray,
Look up, behold the light at play.
For in the storm, a gift is found,
A rainbow rising from the ground.

fairytale

⚜

From the darkness of the past,
　　A wounded heart that cannot last,
　　But hope still flickers like a flame,
　　A light that healing can reclaim.

Though pain may linger, deep and strong,
　　And memories haunt us all day long,
　　There is a path that we can take,
　　A journey to heal, to love, to make.

With courage, we can face our fears,
　　And let our pain flow out like tears,
　　To find the strength we need inside,
　　And know that we are not denied.

We seek a healer for our soul,
　　A trusted guide to make us whole,
　　To teach us how to love and trust,

And heal the wounds that lie in rust.

Through tears and laughter, pain and joy,
 We'll find a path that we employ,
 To leave behind the darkness past,
 And heal the wounds that cannot last.

So let us journey on, dear friend,
 And trust that we will find the end,
 A place of peace and joy and light,
 Where healing blooms in colors bright.

bloom

We bloom and grow like flowers in the spring,
  Reaching up towards the warmth that summer bring.

We spread our petals wide and bask in the light,
  Drinking in the rain and soaking up the bright.

Our roots go deep into the earth below,
  Drawing strength and nourishment to help us grow.

We sway and dance in the gentle breeze,
  And sing a song of joy and gratitude, please.

For we are part of nature's grand design,
  A beautiful creation, both yours and mine.

So let us bloom and grow with all our might,
  And make the world a more beautiful sight.

stormy sea

The clouds hang heavy in the sky,
   A gray veil, like a mournful sigh.
   My thoughts feel just as bleak,
   A jumble of emotions, feeling weak.

The trees are whipped by winds that seem to know
   My inner turmoil and unrest below.
   Lost in chaos, like a ship set free,
   Adrift on the raging, stormy sea.

The world seems to be moving on,
   But I'm stuck, feeling withdrawn.
   The clouds overhead mirror my mood,
   A sense of gloom that can't be subdued.

I long for the sun's warm embrace,
   To banish the clouds and brighten this place.
   But for now, I'll weather this storm,

And hope that soon, I'll feel transformed.

so sweet

In the middle of the night, at the age of seventeen,
I sat alone, in the dark, wondering why.
Without words, I asked myself: Why?
Without words, I answered: Because.
I had to know the reasons, but I didn't.
I had to ask, but I didn't.
And then I fell asleep.
When I woke up the next day, I remembered nothing about
it at all.

imposter syndrome

I am not who I claim to be,
An imposter, I often see.
I wear a mask, a false front,
And fear one day I'll be found out.

Inside, I struggle with self-doubt,
A nagging voice that never gets drowned out.
I question my abilities and worth,
As if I don't belong on this earth.

I compare myself to those around,
And in their success, I feel drowned.
I wonder how they got so far,
While I'm left behind, with a scar.

But I know that it's just a state of mind,
And not a truth that I should bind.
I'll remind myself, every single day,

That I am capable in every way.

And even if I stumble and fall,
   I'll rise again, and stand tall.
   For in the end, it's not about perfection,
   But about progress and self-reflection.

morning dew

In the quiet of the morning, the world begins anew,
  clouds dancing in the sky a good preview,
  of what is to come, a full day ahead,
  thoughts wander places I'd rather not tread.

I push them down, deep inside,
  today will be a great day, I decide.
  The sun rises higher, its warmth on my face,
  a feeling of hope, a sense of grace.

The morning dew glistens on the grass,
  a new beginning, a chance to amass
  all that I desire, all that I dream,
  the possibilities endless, or so it seems.

I take a deep breath, and let it out slow,
  my heart beats steady, ready to go.
  The world is my oyster, my canvas to paint,

and I am the artist, with no restraint.

In the quiet of the morning, I feel alive,
   ready to embrace whatever may arrive.
   For today is a gift, and I will make it count,
   with each step forward, my fears surmount.

So I walk with purpose, and I walk with pride,
   my head held high, my doubts set aside.
   For in the quiet of the morning, I have found,
   the strength to conquer, to be unbound.

high tides

As the tides shift, new treasures are revealed,
 Yet, so much is still concealed.
 The unknown hangs in the air,
 like a pile of clothes on a chair.

As whispers of secrets softly sway,
 Unveiling truths along the way.
 A dance of shadows, a game of light,
 A journey through the shroud of night.

In mysteries draped, we take our stride,
 With courage as our trusted guide.
 For in the depths of the unseen,
 Lies wonders yet to be foreseen.

Like stars that twinkle in the skies,
 Or dreams that in our hearts arise,
 The answers, too, shall soon unfold,

In time's embrace, their tales retold.

So let us venture forth and seek,
Through valleys low and mountains peak,
With curiosity as our flare,
To uncover what lies beyond the air.

With every step, a tale unfurls,
Like petals of a flower that swirls,
And in this journey, we declare,
The beauty found in the unknown's lair.

So as the tides continue to shift,
With every wave and every drift,
Embrace the mysteries in the air,
For they are gifts beyond compare.

wandering freely

In the realm of restless dreams, I wander lost,
A young soul adrift, seeking at any cost,
To grasp the essence of my identity,
Yet finding only echoes of uncertainty.

Oh, how the weight of the world does press upon,
This heart, weary and burdened, all hopes withdrawn,
For in the vast tapestry of existence,
I am but a thread lost in the resistance.

Through tangled paths and labyrinthine mazes,
I tread on shadows, seeking purpose that amazes,
But alas, the mirror reflects a fractured soul,
Whose reflection seems beyond my own control.

I've journeyed far and wide, searching for a sign,
A flicker of truth, a moment so divine,
Yet the more I quest, the more I feel estranged,

As if my soul were destined to be forever changed.

Who am I, but a whisper in the wind,
  A fragile vessel with a spirit trapped within,
  Yearning to break free from these shackles of doubt,
  To discover the truth that I can't live without.

I gaze upon the world with curious eyes,
  Observing lives filled with dreams that touch the skies,
  But mine, a puzzle left unfinished, unclear,
  As I stumble through the fog of my own fear.

In the realm of expectation, I am confined,
  As society weaves its web, tightly entwined,
  Dictating the paths I must take, the roles I must play,
  Leaving little room for my own voice to have a say.

But deep within my core, a flicker of fire ignites,
  A spark of defiance, a yearning that invites,
  To shed the mask society so deems fit,
  And embrace the truth that lies beneath the grit.

For it is in the crucible of struggle and despair,
  That the seeds of self-discovery find their rare,
  Opportunity to bloom and grow, to transform,
  Into a beacon of light, weathering life's storm.

So I embrace the darkness that wraps me tight,
  For in its depths, I find strength to ignite,
  The ember of my spirit, burning with desire,
  To emerge from the ashes, fueling a soul on fire.

With each uncertain step, I unravel the maze,
   Embracing the complexities, no longer a haze,
   For it is through the journey, lost yet found,
   That I reclaim the fragments and stand on solid ground.

And though the road ahead may still be unclear,
   I'll navigate the depths with courage, void of fear,
   For in the realm of self-discovery, I'll reside,
   Embracing my essence with unyielding pride.

So let me wander, let me stumble and explore,
   For it is in this chaos that I'll find what I adore,
   A tapestry woven from fragments and shards,
   A masterpiece reflecting life's intricate regard.

And when I look upon the mirror once more,
   I'll see the culmination of the struggles I bore,
   A young soul no longer lost, but fiercely bright,
   With an identity molded by a courageous fight.

oh my heart

In shadows deep, my doubts take hold,
   A whispered tale of worth untold.
   I linger in the land of "not enough,"
   Where dreams and hopes can seem so tough.

The weight of judgment, heavy on my chest,
   Inadequacy, a cruel and relentless guest.
   Comparisons haunt my every thought,
   A constant battle that can't be fought.

But in this darkness, a flicker remains,
   A gentle reminder of inner flames.
   For within me lies a spirit true,
   A light that shines, breaking through.

No measure defines my heart's embrace,
   Nor standards dictate my rightful place.
   For I am more than doubts may say,

In my own unique and splendid way.

I'll rise above these thoughts unkind,
  Embrace my worth, my soul aligned.
  In self-acceptance, I will thrive,
  Knowing I'm enough, and I'll survive.

living for hope

In the realm of dreams, where desires reside,
   There lies a secret path for you to stride.
   Amidst the chaos, a whisper soft and clear,
   Beckoning you to embrace what's held dear.

Cast off the chains of societal demands,
   For living for others often ties our hands.
   It's time to awaken, to break the mold,
   And let your spirit flourish, free and bold.

Living for yourself, oh what a notion,
   To honor your soul and embrace the potion
   Of self-discovery, a journey untold,
   Where authenticity takes centerfold.

Release the doubts that once held you tight,
   Embrace your passions with unyielding might.
   For in your heart's chamber, a fire burns,

Yearning to explore and take its turn.

Seek the mountains that call to your soul,
  Or wander through meadows, letting time unroll.
  Embrace the ocean's rhythm, wild and free,
  Or dance under moonlight, just you and thee.

Let your laughter echo in the boundless sky,
  As you paint the canvas of your life, oh so high.
  Savor the flavors of life's sweet embrace,
  And let each moment be a sacred space.

In solitude, find solace and peace,
  A sanctuary where your spirit finds release.
  For self-love blooms when you're unafraid,
  To live for yourself, by your own serenade.

Embrace your dreams, for they hold the key,
  To unlock the doors of your destiny.
  No longer bound by others' expectations,
  You discover your own profound revelations.

Living for yourself, a path less trodden,
  Yet within its embrace, your soul will be sodden,
  With joy and purpose, with strength untold,
  As you step into a life that's truly your own.

So, dear wanderer, take the leap, be free,
  Unveil the truth that only you can see.
  Embrace the power that lies deep within,
  And let your life's symphony truly begin.

For in the pursuit of your heart's desire,
    You'll find a flame that never will expire.
    Living for yourself, a melody profound,
    Resounding through the universe, resolute and sound.

track of a love struck girl

The first time their eyes met
   he looked at the floor
   and she felt like a fool.
   The second time their eyes met
   he looked away
   and she felt like a fool.
   The third time their eyes met
   he was looking elsewhere
   and she felt like a fool.
   And then, the fourth time their eyes met,
   he looked at her, and held her gaze.
   She felt like a queen.

Bittersweet Echoes: Nurturing Necessity, Yearning

In the realm of tender hearts, a tale unfolds,
  Of a teenage girl, with secrets yet untold.
  Her spirit danced with hope, love's ember lit,
  But fate played cruelly, where dreams were unfit.

Her eyes, like stars, held a yearning so deep,
  Love's sweet nectar, she yearned to taste and keep.
  In her heart's sanctuary, a boy she adored,
  But his eyes sought elsewhere, love's path ignored.

With every stolen glance, her soul took flight,
  But his affections wandered, out of sight.
  She painted sunsets with his name in gold,
  While her own heartache silently took hold.

Each word she spoke, a serenade of love,

But he remained deaf, and never looked above.
She wove her dreams, like delicate lace,
But his gaze betrayed her, a vacant space.

Her laughter echoed like a crystal chime,
Yet his laughter joined another, marking time.
Her heart, like petals, slowly wilted away,
In the shadowed garden where love couldn't sway.

She battled whispers of self-doubt and fear,
As longing tears carved rivers, crystal clear.
But in her tender spirit, resilience bloomed,
For unrequited love can't be forever doomed.

With time's gentle touch, wounds begin to heal,
She rediscovered strength, her soul made of steel.
She turned the pages, embracing her worth,
Realizing love's value is found in self-rebirth.

Her love may linger in the echoes of the past,
But her heart soared high, the pain didn't last.
For she's a tapestry woven with grace,
A teenage girl's journey, a story to embrace.

And as she grew, love's beauty did unfold,
New chapters written, her spirit ever-bold.
She cherished the lesson, bittersweet yet true,
That loving oneself is where true joy accrues.

In the tapestry of life, her colors will shine,
Her heart, resilient, will learn to intertwine.

For in the depths of unrequited love's sting,
She found her own voice and the strength to sing.

curiosity

In lands where shadows softly dance,
  A trait divine, a daring stance,
  Curiosity takes its graceful flight,
  A spark that kindles in the night.

A flame that burns with fervent grace,
  It lights the path to the unknown space,
  With eyes aglow and heart aflutter,
  Seeking truths that others shutter.

Through pages old and starlit skies,
  Curiosity dares to analyze,
  Unraveling mysteries, threads untwined,
  In the corridors of the curious mind.

What lies beyond that distant star?
  Or in the whispers from afar?
  The curious soul will ever quest,

In pursuit of knowledge, it's truly blessed.

With open heart and open mind,
 Curiosity, so wondrously designed,
 It leads us to discoveries anew,
 Guiding us to sceneries so far askew.

So let us nurture this flame within,
 Embrace the quest that will begin,
 For curiosity's journey has no end,
 A wondrous path on which we'll mend.

the tale of heart shaped jewelry

In the realm of love, a poignant tale I'll share,
  Of letting go, believing it would repair.
  They say, "If you love something, let it be free,
  And if it returns, it's where it's meant to be."

I embraced this wisdom, like a gentle breeze,
  Releasing love with faith, hoping it would appease.
  My heart whispered softly, "Go forth, set it free,
  For love, like a bird, will return, you will see."

With trembling hands, I bid farewell, so sincere,
  Unleashed the affection, suppressing the fear.
  I watched it soar, like a soaring dove in flight,
  Believing true love would return, shining bright.

Days turned to nights, and the nights into years,
  But my love never came back, despite my tears.
  The emptiness gnawed at my weary soul,

As doubts and questions took their heavy toll.

I gazed at the sky, where once we dreamed as one,
   Now clouded by doubts, the damage was done.
   The notion of love's return had faltered and died,
   A bitter truth, a love lost, I couldn't hide.

Yet, in this sorrow, a lesson revealed,
   That love's not a game where fate can be sealed.
   For love has its freedom, it chooses its way,
   Sometimes it won't come back, no matter what you say.

And so I accept, with a heavy heart's ache,
   That love's flight may lead to a different fate.
   But I won't let bitterness erode my soul,
   For love's beauty, once cherished, made me whole.

Though love may not return, as I hoped it would,
   I'll cherish the memories, the times that were good.
   For love's essence lingers, even if it's gone,
   And its whispered echoes shall forever live on.

So let love be free, for it knows its own flight,
   And if it departs, don't let hope lose its light.
   For in the letting go, we find strength anew,
   To love again, and embrace a love that's true.

life's great tapestry

In the tapestry of life's grand design,
  A quest begins, where hearts align.
  Amidst the chaos, a sacred thread weaves,
  A dance of destiny, where two souls conceive.

In the realm of dreams and whispered sighs,
  A yearning stirs, seeking love's sweet ties.
  Across vast oceans and mountains tall,
  Destiny beckons, heed love's call.

Through countless seasons and lonely nights,
  A search commences, chasing love's delights.
  In fleeting moments, a glimpse we see,
  A flicker of hope, our hearts set free.

Through crowded streets and empty spaces,
  We journey on, tracing ethereal traces.
  In every encounter, a chance may arise,

To lock eyes with love, a soul's surprise.

A meeting ordained, as if by fate's decree,
   Two souls collide, their spirits set free.
   In the depths of gazes, secrets unfold,
   As hearts entwine, a story yet untold.

Time unravels its mysterious course,
   Two souls entwined, entangled, and endorsed.
   Through joy and sorrow, love's symphony plays,
   A soulmate's presence, a guiding blaze.

In moments of silence, a language unknown,
   Their souls converse, a resonance grown.
   Through understanding, they find their place,
   Completing each other, with love's embrace.

With every laugh, a melody bright,
   In every tear shed, a shared plight.
   Hand in hand, they navigate life's trails,
   Bound by love's covenant, where passion prevails.

Through life's great tapestry, they are one,
   A soulmate's journey, forever begun.
   With every heartbeat, a rhythm divine,
   They found each other, in love's grand design.

do you know what it feels like?

Do you know what it feels like?
   To be a whole world that nobody knows?
   Do you know what it's like to love, and to grieve, and to write, and then to be forgotten?
   I'd ask you if it hurts. But I already know the answer.
   Do you know what it feels like?
   To be a whole world that nobody knows?

flabbergasted

In realms of awe where minds collide,
   Flabbergasted hearts take a wild ride.
   A symphony of wonder and surprise,
   Unveiling visions before our eyes.

A twist of fate, a turn so sly,
   Leaves us speechless, wondering why.
   Stars dance in the midnight sky,
   Leaving us flabbergasted, oh my!

Life's mysteries, a puzzle's grace,
   Etching awe on every face.
   With eyes aglow, we stand amassed,
   In flabbergasted moments that forever last.

simple and easy

Love,
   an enigma,
   a whirlwind of emotions,
   a dance of the heart,
   unfolding in unpredictable ways.

It knows no boundaries,
   no rules or restrictions,
   it transcends time and space,
   defying logic,
   igniting passions deep within.

Love,
   a gentle touch,
   a soft embrace,
   a whisper in the dark,
   a symphony of souls,
   melding into one.

It blooms like a flower,
   fragile yet resilient,
   nurtured by connection,
   watered by understanding,
   and rooted in vulnerability.

Love,
   a cosmic force,
   binding us together,
   uniting hearts,
   across oceans and continents,
   in a tapestry of shared moments.

It can heal wounds,
   mend brokenness,
   and bring light to the darkest corners,
   filling empty spaces,
   with warmth and tenderness.

Love,
   a masterpiece,
   painted with colors unseen,
   crafted with words unspoken,
   expressed in gestures,
   and felt in the depths of our being.

It is a gift,
   to be cherished and cherished,
   an endless journey,
   of discovery and growth,
   a treasure to be found.

Love,
    an ever-changing melody,
    played on the strings of the heart,
    evoking joy, passion, and pain,
    teaching us to love ourselves,
    and each other, unconditionally.

So, let love guide you,
    let it be your compass,
    as you navigate this world,
    for love is the essence,
    that makes life truly worth living.

soulmates

In the vast expanse of time and space,
  Two souls were destined to embrace.
  They sought each other, near and far,
  Bound by a connection, like a shooting star.

No rhyme or reason could explain,
  The depth of love that would sustain.
  A cosmic union, an eternal flame,
  Two souls entwined, never to be the same.

Through lifetimes and dimensions they would roam,
  Searching for solace, a place to call home.
  In the chaos of existence, they found a space,
  A sanctuary of love, their hearts could embrace.

They danced through the cosmos, hand in hand,
  A symphony of souls, a celestial band.
  In every lifetime, they'd find their way,

Guided by destiny, come what may.

No distance or time could ever divide,
   The bond they shared, so deep inside.
   They were soul mates, destined to be,
   A love story written in the stars, for all to see.

Through the trials and tribulations they'd face,
   Their love would never waver, nor erase.
   For they were connected, heart and soul,
   A love so pure, it made them whole.

So, cherish the soul mate that you find,
   A love that's rare, one of a kind.
   For in this vast universe, we're blessed,
   To find a soul mate, our heart's true nest.

danger

On the edge of existence, I teeter and sway,
In the twilight of uncertainty, I find my way.
Life's a daring tightrope, a precarious dance,
A delicate balance of fate and chance.

I walk on the precipice of dreams and despair,
With each step I take, I'm aware and aware.
The abyss below, a chasm so deep,
Yet I stride forward, my secrets to keep.

In the realm of the unknown, I make my stand,
With courage as my compass, in this vast, wild land.
I taste the thrill of every moment, so raw,
Embracing the chaos, embracing the flaw.

Living on the edge, I find my release,
In the chaos and madness, I discover my peace.
With every heartbeat, with every breath,

danger

I journey through life, on the edge of death.

For it's here on this edge, where life truly begins,
   Where the soul finds its fire, and the spirit wins.
   In the maelstrom of passion, in the storm of desire,
   I live life on the edge, where dreams catch fire.

So, let me dance on this tightrope, let me take flight,
   In the realm of the unknown, I'll find my light.
   For it's on the edge, I'm truly alive,
   Where I learn to embrace, where I learn to survive.

chasing the high of happiness

Chasing the high of happiness, I am a seeker in a world of colors.
A kaleidoscope of emotions, I chase that elusive butterfly.

In the sun-kissed meadows of laughter, I run with outstretched arms,
Trying to catch the fleeting moments, the joy that dances just out of reach.

I chase the high of happiness, through fields of dreams and moonlit nights.
I follow the whispers of my heart, to where the stars ignite.

With every breath, I inhale hope, exhale the weight of sorrows past.
Chasing the high, I climb the mountains, seeking the summit where joy will last.

In the warmth of a lover's embrace, in the laughter of friends

around,
  I find the echoes of ecstasy, in the simple joys that I've found.

But happiness is a wily creature, eluding capture, slipping through fingers.
  Yet, in the chase, I find the journey, in the pursuit, I discover the singers.

For life is a symphony of moments, each note, a step in the dance.
  And as I chase the high of happiness, I find it's the pursuit that gives life a chance.

So, I'll chase that high with a heart ablaze, through valleys and peaks, I'll roam.
  For in the chase, I find my purpose, in the pursuit of happiness, I find my home.

this is what dreams are made of

In the depths of the night,
   where shadows dance in moonlight,
   lies the secret to ignite,
   the fire within your sight.

Follow your dreams, they say,
   like birds soaring through the day,
   unfettered by doubt's sway,
   in pursuit of a destined way.

Fear may whisper in your ear,
   fill your heart with doubt and fear,
   but don't succumb, my dear,
   for dreams are meant to persevere.

Embrace the unknown,
   where passions are sown,
   and let your spirit be shown,

in dreams that are yours alone.

The journey may be tough,
  with detours and rebuffs,
  but keep your dreams enough,
  and they will guide you through rough.

Unleash the boundless you,
  let your dreams come into view,
  for life's canvas is anew,
  when dreams become what you do.

So dare to take the leap,
  from slumber to the peak,
  and let your dreams speak,
  of the life you long to seek.

For in following your dreams,
  in the realms of endless streams,
  you'll find joy in sunbeams,
  and fulfillment beyond extremes.

ode to the journey

Loving life is an art, a masterpiece of the heart,
  A canvas painted with moments, a work of living art.
  It's the sunrise's gentle kiss on the morning's cheek,
  The whispered secrets of the wind, so mild and meek.

It's the taste of laughter, sweet on the lips,
  The warmth of friendships, in the heart's eclipse.
  Loving life is a dance, a rhythm so free,
  A melody of moments, a symphony to be.

It's the embrace of nature, the kiss of the sun,
  The feeling of belonging, when day is done.
  It's the thrill of the journey, the unknown's call,
  The courage to rise, the will to stand tall.

Loving life is a tapestry woven with threads,
  Of joy and sorrow, of dreams and their spreads.
  It's the gratitude for every breath we take,

The love we give and the love we make.

In the beauty of a flower, in the twinkle of a star,
In the depths of our souls, no matter how far,
Loving life is a treasure, a gift so divine,
A celebration of existence, in every single line.

So cherish each moment, with a heart open wide,
In the ebb and flow of life's changing tide.
For in the embrace of love, both big and small,
Lies the truest essence of loving life, after all.

starlight

In the realm of dreams, I build my world,
  A tapestry of hopes, unfurled.
  With each sunrise, a canvas anew,
  Living my dream life, bold and true.

A life where passion knows no bounds,
  In the symphony of life, my heart resounds.
  With purpose as my guiding star,
  I live my dream life, near and far.

No shackles of doubt, no chains of fear,
  In this dream life, I hold what's dear.
  With open arms and eyes wide gleam,
  I live my life, it's not a dream.

all of us

We are all related
   by the decay of our bodies.
   The blush on a rose,
   the red glow of a sunset—
   tears and blood.
   We are all related
   by the pain in our bodies,
   the shame, the longing, the fear:
   all the ways we fail to speak.

the kiss

In a world where time dances on the breeze,
   A tale of love unfolds with graceful ease.
   It begins with a glance, a fleeting affair,
   Love at first sight, beyond compare.

In a crowded room or beneath starry skies,
   Two souls collide, a sweet surprise.
   Eyes lock in a moment, hearts ignite,
   A connection forged in that fateful night.

Invisible threads of destiny weave,
   Binding two hearts, causing them to believe.
   That love can bloom in the blink of an eye,
   As if written by fate up in the sky.

It's not just the physical, it's something more,
   A connection of spirits at its core.
   A feeling so deep, it defies explanation,

the kiss

Love at first sight, a divine revelation.

In each other's presence, time stands still,
   As if the universe conspired to fulfill,
   The dreams of two souls meant to be,
   Bound together for all eternity.

Though skeptics may doubt this romantic delight,
   There's a magic in love at first sight.
   For in that moment, a story begins,
   A love that conquers all, as the universe grins.

So cherish the moments when eyes first meet,
   For love at first sight is bittersweet.
   A gift from the heavens, a beautiful sight,
   A love that burns brightly, forever alight.

workaholic

I've got a lot of work to do
    maybe I'll see you later, right now I've got a lot of work to do
    I have a lot of work to do
    I have an immense amount of work to do
    I have a lot of work to do
    I have a lot of work to do
    maybe I'll see you later, right now I've got a lot of work to do

the beautiful inside of you

In the quiet spaces of your soul's embrace,
　Where truth and kindness interlace,
　There lies a beauty, pure and true,
　The radiant light that's born in you.

Beyond the surface, where eyes may see,
　A depth of wonder, a mystery,
　In the chambers of your beating heart,
　A masterpiece of precious art.

No mirror reflects this inner grace,
　No portrait captures its tender trace,
　For it's the beauty that dwells within,
　A timeless treasure, a sacred sin.

In laughter's echo and tears that flow,
　In every kindness you bestow,
　In every dream that you pursue,

Resides the beautiful inside of you.

In the strength that rises when you're weak,
In the words you choose when others speak,
In the love that overflows and grows,
Your inner beauty truly shows.

It's not the skin, the form, the face,
But your spirit's warmth, its gentle grace,
That makes you radiant, kind, and true,
Oh, the beautiful inside of you.

In the quiet moments, when you reflect,
In the love you give and never neglect,
In the way you lift others when they're down,
You wear your beauty like a crown.

So remember this as you go your way,
Let your inner beauty guide each day,
For it's the light that forever shines,
A testament to your soul's design.

Embrace the beauty inside your core,
Let it shine brighter than ever before,
For it's a gift to cherish and renew,
The beautiful inside of you.

rock beach

Beneath the bright blue sky, we stand,
  Upon a shore of stones, hand in hand.
  Each pebble polished by the timeless sea,
  A testament to nature's artistry.

The waves, like poets, whisper in our ears,
  Their tales of distant lands and ancient years.
  They sing of voyages and dreams untold,
  As we search for treasures in the pebbles' fold.

The rocks beneath our feet, both smooth and rough,
  Tell stories of endurance, strong and tough.
  They've weathered storms and tides with quiet grace,
  A silent testament to time and place.

Seagulls soar above with wings outspread,
  Their cries like echoes of the sea's own thread.
  They dance upon the breeze with perfect ease,

A ballet of freedom beneath the endless seas.

As twilight paints the sky in hues of gold,
    We watch the ocean's secrets slowly unfold.
    The world dissolves, and we become the shore,
    Lost in the beauty of this place we adore.

So let us linger here, you and I,
    Beneath the boundless, starlit, open sky.
    Upon this rock-strewn beach, our spirits soar,
    In nature's embrace, forevermore.

Phoebe

In the faded photographs, your beauty shines like a beacon
   A beacon that has guided me through the years
   Through the ups and downs, the twists and turns of life
   You are like a lighthouse, always there to guide me home

But now, you are gone, and all I have left are the memories
   Memories of your laughter, your wit, and your love
   You were more than just a grandmother to me
   You were a friend, a confidant, and a mentor
   You taught me to be strong and independent
   To stand tall and proud no matter what people said

You were beautiful inside and out,
   And I know that you will always be with me,
   Guiding me through life's storms,
   As my lighthouse in the dark.

So here's to you, Phoebe,

My beautiful great-grandmother,
The woman who shaped me into who I am today.
You may be gone, but your memory will live in me forever.

the first night

Beneath the canvas of a starry sky,
   Two souls embarked, no longer shy,
   Upon a journey, fate designed,
   The first night of love, forever entwined.

A cafe, dimly lit, where they did meet,
   Nervous smiles, hearts skipped a beat,
   Their eyes locked in a timeless gaze,
   A connection formed in mysterious ways.

Conversations flowed like a gentle stream,
   Dreams and secrets, they began to gleam,
   Their laughter danced in the candlelight,
   On this first night, everything felt so right.

As the evening wore on, time stood still,
   No longer searching, they'd found their fill,
   In each other's company, they found their grace,

The world outside faded, in this sacred space.

They shared their stories, their hopes, their fears,
    Laying bare their souls, wiping away tears,
    A soulmate connection, rare and true,
    In the hush of the night, their love grew.

Hand in hand, they strolled through the park,
    Under the moon's soft, silver arc,
    Whispers of love, promises to keep,
    The first night of a love so deep.

As the clock chimed midnight, they knew,
    Their souls had found a love that's true,
    A bond that time could not erase,
    The first night of their eternal embrace.

In the first night's magic, destiny had its say,
    Two soulmates destined to find their way,
    Through the journey of life, side by side,
    Forever in love, with hearts open wide.

for my love

To my dearest love, my heart's true guide,
In your embrace, my soul finds its stride,
With every sunrise and the setting sun,
Our love's journey is never done.

Through the trials of life, hand in hand,
Together we stand, an unbreakable band,
In your eyes, I see the endless sea,
Of love and devotion you hold for me.

Your laughter, a melody that brightens my day,
Your love, a constant, in every way,
In your smile, I find my greatest treasure,
A love so deep, it knows no measure.

Through the years, our love has grown,
A love so deep, it's become our home,
In your presence, I find my peace,

A love like ours will never cease.

Through the storms and the gentle breeze,
Our love's grown stronger, with such ease,
For you are my anchor in life's vast sea,
My love, forever and always, you'll be.

With you, my love, my heart has found,
A love so profound, so perfectly bound,
In your arms, I've discovered my place,
Forever and always, in your embrace.

So here's to us, my beloved dear,
Through every joy and every tear,
With all my heart, I'll forever say,
I love you more with each passing day.

lost soul

In shadows deep, a tale untold,
A heartache deep, a loss untold,
A journey fraught, a soul untold,
The story of a lost soul, I'll unfold.

In the quiet hush of a mother's dream,
A life once bloomed, a tender gleam,
But Fate's cruel hand, in silence unseen,
Took away a child, like a fleeting beam.

Innocence lost, a cradle left bare,
A mother's sorrow, too heavy to bear,
A father's tears, a world unfair,
Aching hearts in the depths of despair.

A tiny soul, too pure to stay,
Wings of angels carried it away,
To a place of peace, where it will play,

In eternal sunshine, night and day.

Though the pain is deep, and tears may flow,
    The love remains, an eternal glow,
    In memories cherished, where dreams still grow,
    In the heart's embrace, where love's rivers flow.

For though this journey took an unexpected toll,
    The love for this lost soul, forever whole,
    In the gentle winds, in each whispered shoal,
    We find solace for the lost, eternal soul.

college days

In the realm of knowledge, we set our gaze,
 To navigate the labyrinth of college days,
 A journey of struggle, both night and dawn,
 As we tread the path, sometimes feeling drawn.

With backpacks heavy, and hearts unsure,
 We ventured forth, seeking wisdom pure,
 Amidst lecture halls and libraries vast,
 The challenges ahead, so daunting they cast.

The syllabus, a mountain, we aimed to climb,
 Beneath the weight of deadlines, we'd chime,
 But in every struggle, we found our way,
 Growing stronger, wiser, day by day.

Sleepless nights, with textbooks as our guide,
 Burning the midnight oil, side by side,
 For exams loomed large, like stormy skies,

Yet, we persevered, reaching for the prize.

Friendships forged in the crucible of stress,
    Through highs and lows, we'd assess,
    The strength in unity, the bonds we'd share,
    In the tapestry of college life, so rare.

Financial woes and loans to bear,
    The cost of dreams, a burden we'd wear,
    But in these trials, we'd find our grace,
    As we strive to create a better place.

From lectures to labs, and seminars so grand,
    Our minds expanded across the land,
    For in the struggle of college's haze,
    We uncovered our potential, in myriad ways.

So, raise a toast to college days,
    To the trials, the lessons, in countless ways,
    For in the struggle, we found our might,
    In the pursuit of knowledge, burning bright.

buzz buzz

In the realm of whispers, shadows cast,
   A tale unfolds, spreading far and fast,
   Through the grapevine of secrets, it flies,
   Invisible wings, in the form of lies.

Buzz, buzz, the rumors take flight,
   Like bees in a garden, in the warm sunlight,
   They dance through the air, a frenzied swarm,
   Spreading gossip's venom, causing harm.

Innocent words, they twist and turn,
   As they travel from ear to ear, they churn,
   Into monstrous tales, so distorted and vast,
   As truth and fiction blur, in the gossip's blast.

A careless word, a thoughtless jest,
   Can fan the flames, create unrest,
   The stories grow, with each retell,

A tangled web of truths and lies, they swell.

Yet, in this chaos, let us beware,
    For gossip's sting, it's not just air,
    It tarnishes reputations, friendships fray,
    Leaving scars that never truly fade away.

So, before you join the buzz's grand parade,
    Pause and consider the price that's paid,
    For the truth and kindness should prevail,
    Over gossip's allure, let compassion sail.

Let us strive for words that uplift and mend,
    Not contribute to the gossip's bitter end,
    In the quiet of our hearts, let wisdom weigh,
    The power of words, and what they convey.

In the world of whispers, let us choose,
    To break the cycle, not to abuse,
    The trust we share, in the bonds we keep,
    For in silence or speech, our integrity runs deep.

Buzz, buzz, may we always remember,
    The harm that gossip can kindle and engender,
    And seek instead, in our daily quest,
    To spread kindness and truth, in words that are blessed.

deaf ears

In shadows cast, I weave my tale,
   A whispered truth, a fragile sail,
   But in the eyes that meet my plea,
   Doubt's heavy shroud envelopes me.

I speak my heart, I lay it bare,
   Yet disbelief hangs in the air,
   Like storm clouds dark, they gather near,
   And all my words fall on deaf ears.

I've walked a path of honest grace,
   But still, they question my embrace,
   The doubt, it lingers, like a ghost,
   A haunting specter, I fear the most.

Innocence in my voice may ring,
   Yet they suspect some hidden thing,
   My earnest words, they will deceive,

A skeptic's heart is hard to relieve.

But truth endures, like dawn's first light,
   Emerging from the darkest night,
   Though doubters may their doubts conceive,
   In time, my innocence they'll perceive.

For honesty is a beacon's glow,
   A steady flame that soon will show,
   The falsehoods from the truth's reprieve,
   And in the end, they'll all believe.

rest and relaxation

In the quietude of evening's embrace,
   When daylight fades with a gentle grace,
   I seek the solace of a tranquil shore,
   Where relaxation's waves forever pour.

Beneath the stars' soft, twinkling light,
   I let go of worries, take flight,
   Into a realm of serenity and peace,
   Where life's incessant struggles cease.

A hammock sways in the gentle breeze,
   Whispering secrets among the trees,
   As nature's lullaby softly sings,
   A melody of calm that gently clings.

The world, once bustling, now recedes,
   As my heart and mind find what it needs,
   To unwind, release, and let go,

In this tranquil moment, my spirit will grow.

With every breath of the cool night air,
I cast away burdens, I release despair,
For in the art of relaxation's grace,
I find my sanctuary, my sacred space.

So close your eyes and let troubles fade,
In the realm of relaxation, they'll be unmade,
In the stillness of this peaceful night,
Find your refuge, your soul's delight.

I like you

I like you, I like you, I like you
   I like the way you say no, I like the way you say yes
   I like the way you are, I like the way you aren't
   I like your two left feet and all your other feet too
   I like the way you smile and I like the way you don't
   I like you, I like you, I like you

late night dreamer

In this world of games, there is no place for
me. There must be rules, there must be limits;
there must be winners and losers. But when
you dream, your world is the game, and in that
world you are allowed to do everything. To
fly on a magic carpet with your friends, to
vanquish all of your enemies with only the push
of a button, or to leave your home behind and go
exploring for new worlds… these are all things you
can do in a dream. In my dreams I have many
friends. Some live next door and some live far away,
some I see every day and some I don't see very
often. But no matter how close we become or how little
we talk, they will always be there when I need them –
they are my friends.

burnt out flame

In a world ablaze with hope's bright flame,
  I stand alone, lost in despair's cruel game.
  Amidst the laughter, the smiles, and the cheer,
  I find myself drowning in a sea of fear.

For hope is a bird that soars on high,
  But its wings elude me, I cannot fly.
  In the shadows I linger, a soul forlorn,
  In a world where hope's light has been torn.

I search for solace in the darkest night,
  But my heart is shrouded in endless fright.
  The stars above, they twinkle and gleam,
  Yet in my heart, it's a fractured dream.

I see the beauty in each sunrise's hue,
  But it's a fleeting glimpse, a moment too few.
  In this world of hope, I've lost my way,

Trapped in the night, where despair holds sway.

Yet still, I yearn for a glimmer of light,
 A beacon of hope in the endless night.
 For even in darkness, a spark can ignite,
 And guide the lost soul toward hope's resplendent sight.

Though I may stumble, my spirit may bend,
 I'll keep searching for hope around every bend.
 In a world of hope, I'll find my place,
 And the shadows of despair, I'll steadily erase.

For deep within, a flicker remains,
 A ember of hope in the darkest of lanes.
 In this world of hope, I'll learn to cope,
 And find the strength to rise, and once more, to hope.

could I be good enough?

In the quiet depths of self-doubt's domain,
   Lies the phantom of Imposter's haunting refrain.
   A whispering shadow, a relentless tide,
   In the chambers of the mind, it loves to hide.

A masquerade of confidence we feign,
   While battling the specter's ceaseless chain.
   We wear a mask of competence, so skilled,
   Yet beneath it all, our doubts are unfulfilled.

In meetings and stages, we take our place,
   But a nagging voice questions our embrace.
   "Do you belong here?" it taunts and teases,
   Leaving us tangled in doubt's thorny creases.

We see the accomplishments others share,
   And wonder if our success is just thin air.
   Comparisons breed self-doubt's bitter fruit,

As Imposter Syndrome takes root.

But remember, dear soul, it's a common plight,
    This sense of fraudulence we try to fight.
    In the hearts of many, it dwells and thrives,
    A challenge to conquer as our spirit strives.

For in our flaws and doubts, we must confide,
    To break the chains Imposter Syndrome tied.
    Embrace the truth that you're unique and strong,
    In your journey of growth, you truly belong.

You're not an impostor; you're learning to grow,
    A work in progress, letting self-doubt go.
    With courage and patience, you'll find your way,
    And Imposter Syndrome's grip will slowly sway.

So let not the shadow dictate your course,
    You're genuine, unique, a powerful force.
    In this battle against doubt, you're not alone,
    Together we rise, and Imposter Syndrome's overthrown.

festival

Amidst a crowd, yet lost in solitude's embrace,
  I wear a mask to hide my inner space.
  Surrounded by voices, laughter, and cheer,
  But within, a loneliness that's all too clear.

Invisible walls encircle my heart,
  A feeling of isolation, worlds apart.
  I stand among friends, or so it seems,
  But loneliness lingers like haunting dreams.

The chatter surrounds me like a distant stream,
  Yet my thoughts echo in a silent scream.
  I long for connection, a genuine bond,
  In this sea of faces, where do I belong?

It's not the absence of people or their grace,
  But the longing for a deeper, soulful embrace.
  A yearning for hearts to truly entwine,

81

To bridge the gap between your world and mine.

In the midst of the crowd, I seek a friend,
Someone to understand, to comprehend.
To share the burdens that weigh me down,
And turn this solitude into a vibrant town.

Loneliness in company, an ironic art,
A complex feeling tearing at the heart.
But know, dear soul, you're not alone,
In this world of paradoxes, we all have known.

So let's reach out, break down the walls,
Build connections that answer silent calls.
In the midst of people, let love set free,
And banish the shadows of loneliness from thee.

under the sycamore tree

Love's gentle touch, a guiding star,
   In every smile, no matter how far.
   In joy and sorrow, it remains our guide,
   Forever bound, in love, we'll reside.

picnic basket

Beneath the azure, in the sun's warm embrace,
   A couple found their tranquil, secret place.
   With a checkered blanket spread on grassy ground,
   They shared a picnic, love in every sound.

She brought a basket filled with sweet delight,
   He brought his guitar, strumming soft and light.
   As they nibbled on sandwiches and wine,
   Their hearts entwined, a melody divine.

The breeze played notes through leaves of emerald green,
   Their laughter mingled in the sunlit scene.
   In this picnic for two, love's warmth did glow,
   A cherished memory, forever to bestow.

With each bite and each chord, their bond grew strong,
   In nature's arms, where they truly belong.
   Under the sky's canvas, they found their retreat,

picnic basket

A love-filled picnic, a memory sweet.

listen up

In the silence, where the heartstrings softly play,
   There lies a precious gift that brightens up our day.
   It's the feeling of being heard, understood so deep,
   A treasure in our souls, we'll forever keep.

When words find open ears and empathy's embrace,
   The burdens of our hearts find solace, find their place.
   In the presence of a friend, a listening ear so near,
   We find a sanctuary where our doubts and fears disappear.

It's more than just the words we speak aloud,
   It's in the way they listen, in the care they've vowed.
   A connection forged in moments, where silence softly speaks,
   In being truly heard, our spirit finds its peaks.

So, cherish those who lend an empathetic ear,
   For in the act of listening, love and trust appear.
   In the feeling of being heard, a bond is born anew,

A testament to the power of compassion, tried and true.

stinky

In shadows cast, they silently prowl,
  With grace and mystery, they beguile and howl.
  Enigmatic creatures of the night,
  With eyes that gleam, two orbs of radiant light.

Their fur, a canvas of patterns and hue,
  Soft as a whisper, in shades of gray and blue.
  They stalk through moonbeams with a feline grace,
  Invisible footprints on the night's quiet space.

With whiskers keen, they navigate the dark,
  In pursuit of prey, they leave their mark.
  But when the hunt is done, they curl up tight,
  In slumber's embrace, they find their respite.

Independent spirits, they roam and roam,
  Yet find their way back to the place called home.
  They purr and knead, a gentle, soothing sound,

stinky

In the warmth of your lap, contentment is found.

Mysterious and regal, they wear a crown,
    In the kingdom of creatures, they'll never back down.
    The envoys of a world we can't quite see,
    Bring a touch of magic to both you and me.

savannah

In a land where the sky met the sea so vast,
　A honeymoon couple's adventure was cast.
　Hand in hand, they strolled on the golden shore,
　Two hearts entwined, forevermore.

Beneath the radiant sun's warm embrace,
　They found love's refuge, a tranquil place.
　Their laughter echoed in the ocean's song,
　As they danced on the sands, all day long.

The waves whispered secrets to the moonlit night,
　As the couple, under stars, held each other tight.
　Their love, like a lighthouse, guiding their way,
　Through the mysteries of this enchanting bay.

In a secluded cove, they built a fire's glow,
　And shared their dreams in its soft, warm flow.
　They toasted to love with glasses of wine,

Savoring moments that felt so divine.

As dawn painted the sky with shades of pink and gold,
   Their love story continued, a tale to be told.
   In this paradise, they discovered their grace,
   A timeless journey in this sacred space.

Days turned into weeks, their bond grew strong,
   In this haven where they truly belong.
   A honeymoon's promise, forever they'd keep,
   As they sailed into life's ocean, love's ocean so deep.

In the end, the sands and the tides may fade,
   But their love, in their hearts, would never degrade.
   For in this land where the sky met the sea,
   Two souls found a love, pure and free.

About the Author

My name is Allison Van Wheeler. I've been a writer for as long as I can remember - from scribbling in journals as a child to studying creative writing in college. I have worked in various industries but always knew that writing was my true passion. I finally decided to take the leap and pursue a career as an author.

My writing focuses on young adult romance and poetry, and I'm constantly inspired by everything life has to offer. I've published multiple poetry books and a young adult novella and am currently working on my next project. When I'm not writing, you can find me crafting, painting, or playing video games with my husband, Justin. I believe that you get what you give, and I hope that my work reflects that.

Thank you for taking the time to get to know me a little better. I'm excited to share my writing journey with you and hope that my stories and poems bring you joy, inspiration, and a little bit of magic.

You can connect with me on:

- https://www.allisonvanwheeler.com
- https://www.instagram.com/allisonvanwheeler

Milton Keynes UK
Ingram Content Group UK Ltd.
UKHW021915190224
438095UK00006BA/222